I0623916

TEX-MEX COOKING

Jillian Stewart

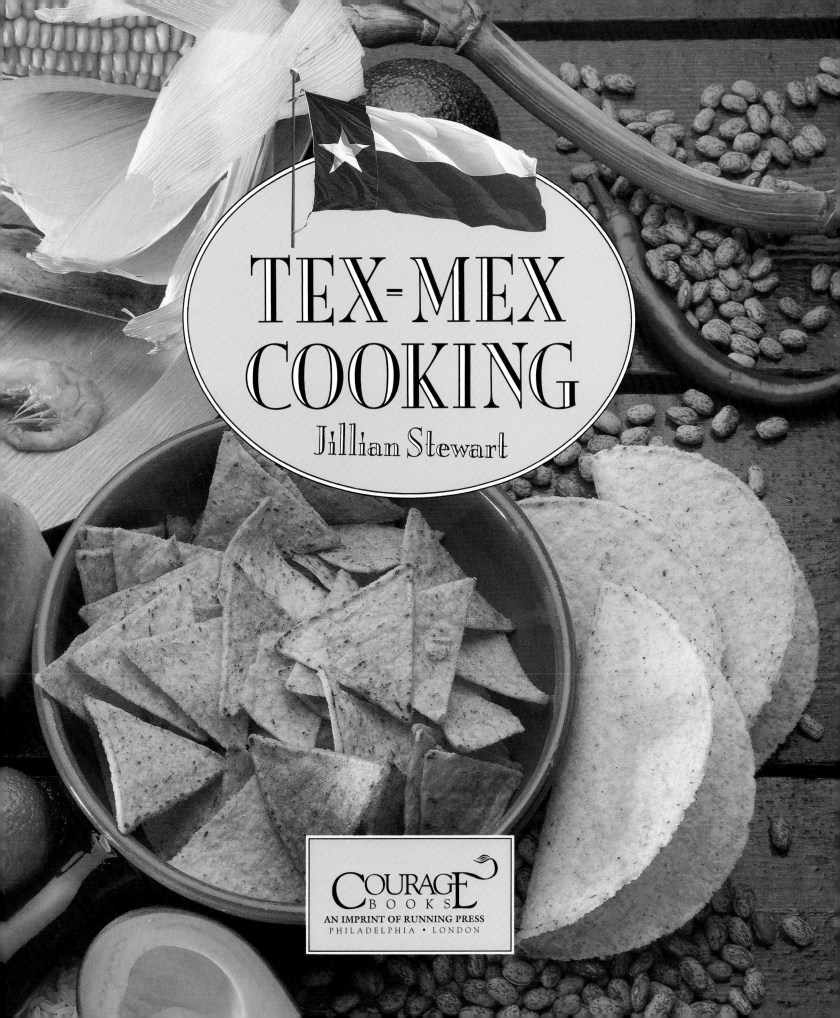

TEX-MEX COOKING

Jillian Stewart

COURAGE BOOKS

AN IMPRINT OF RUNNING PRESS
PHILADELPHIA · LONDON

Copyright © 1994 CLB Publishing
This edition first published in the United States
by Courage Books, an imprint of
Running Press Book Publishers.

All rights reserved. This book may not be
reproduced whole or in part in any form or
by any means, electronic or mechanical,
including photocopying, recording, or by
any information storage or retrieval system not
known or hereafter invented, without
written permission from the publisher and
copyright holders.

CLB 4172
9 8 7 6 5 4 3 2 1
Digit on the right indicates the number of this
printing.

Library of Congress Cataloging-in-Publication
Number 93-87603

ISBN 1-561-38-447-X

This book was designed and produced by
CLB Publishing, Godalming, Surrey, England.

Editor: Jillian Stewart
Introduction: Bill Harris
Designer: Philip Clucas
Picture Researcher: Leora Kahn
Photographers: Neil Sutherland and Peter Barry

Typesetting by Inforum
Printed and bound in Singapore

Published by Courage Books,
an imprint of Running Press Book Publishers
125 South Twenty-second Street
Philadelphia, PA 19103-4399

Contents

Introduction

Above: this photograph from the early 1900s shows children eating watermelon, one of Texas' biggest exports. Right: the Chapel of the Mission San Antonio de Valero, renamed the Alamo in 1800, in San Antonio.

There is hardly a city anywhere in America that doesn't have at least one "Tex-Mex" joint, where burritos and enchiladas often come from the same package without regard for the fact that the former ought to be a filled flour tortilla and the latter made from a corn tortilla. The *pièce de résistance* in nearly all them is what they bill as Texas-style chili, invariably made with hamburger meat, some canned tomatoes, kidney beans, reconstituted onions and prepackaged chili powder. And many of those that have refried beans on their menus obviously get them from a can. The same is often true of the salsa.

But even though salsa in bottles and cans has replaced ketchup as the condiment of choice in America's households, it may be as close as most Americans will ever come to the real joy of border food, the first cousin of Mexican cuisine usually

11

called Tex-Mex. But the good news is that, although no one would ever regret having made the trip, it isn't necessary to go to Brownsville or El Paso to discover the pleasure. The fresh ingredients are available just about anywhere, and the bit of effort it takes to combine them quickly becomes a labor of love which, as any Texan will testify, is what makes all the difference.

Apart from loving care, what usually makes this cooking style memorable is the fruit of the plants of the genus *Capsicum,* whose 200 or more different varieties are known collectively as chiles. The word is used to describe the plant and its pods, but when it is spelled chili, it describes the classic dish made with chiles and meat, usually known in Texas as a "bowl of red." Spelled with an "i" it is also a packaged powder made of chiles, cumin, oregano, salt and garlic usually laced with chemicals to extend its shelf life. Chiles themselves are also interchangeably called "peppers," and we have Christopher Columbus to thank for that.

When he discovered the New World, the Admiral of the Ocean Sea set about naming some of the things he found. That he named the natives "Indians" still raises hackles among the politically correct, but, then, Columbus never claimed to be an anthropologist. He apparently wasn't much of a botanist, either, because in his enthusiasm to prove that he had discovered the Indies, he decided that the chiles he found were a form of the plant that produces black pepper which, as it turns out, isn't even a close relative. It was a self-serving choice of words because back in the 15th century, black pepper was as valuable as gold and it was the prospect of finding a source of it that made funding his voyage seem like a good business proposition in the first place. But he might better have listened a little more closely to the people who met him at the shore. Their neighbors across the Gulf of Mexico, the Nahuatl, had been calling these pungent pods chilli (which archaelogists insist on spelling with a double "l") for generations. Other pre-Columbian cultures had used them as commonly as modern Americans use salt for at least 5,000 years, possibly even longer. And along with corn and beans, chiles were among the first crops that turned prehistoric American hunters into farmers, bringing civilization to the New World.

Chiles can be bought fresh or dried, frozen or canned, but they are as easy to grow as crabgrass.

Most varieties will thrive just about anywhere, even in a pot on a kitchen windowsill. It goes without saying that a little bit goes a long way, and once having introduced the plant into a garden, it is almost as adept at reseeding itself as hollyhocks. As 17th-century Americans grew tomatoes as decorative plants, some of their descendants do the same with chiles, almost all of which are quite beautiful. But if they are a feast for the eyes, they also seem to be among the most healthful fruits available to mankind. They are unusually high in vitamins A, C and E, for instance, and as little as an ounce of chiles provides the recommended minimum daily requirement of all three. Added to this is a recent university study that concluded that chiles are a natural antibiotic whose germ-killing properties may be effective in curing colds and flu. The bottom line seems to be that these colorful pods are good for you. But even if they weren't, they do wonderful things to all kinds of food, turning almost any meal into an adventure and eliminating blandness from our culinary vocabulary.

The dominant characteristic of chiles is their heat, of course, but they also add flavor. Forgetting this, many cooks trying to avoid a palate-searing result sometimes opt for reducing the quantity of chiles called for in a recipe. They shouldn't, not only because it destroys the result by eliminating the important balance of flavor, but because there is a better way. The heat comes from a natural chemical called capasaicin that is generally concentrated in the seeds and the internal ribs of the chile pod, and it can be dramatically reduced by cutting away those parts. Because the seeds and ribs are the source of the heat, it follows that the smaller the chile the hotter it will be because of a greater concentration of capasaicin and a good rule of thumb to avoid excessive heat is to choose bigger chiles.

There are also ways to combat the heat in a chile-laced dish. Down along the Rio Grande, folks will swear that a couple of long-necked bottles of beer will quench the fire, but the fact is that alcohol actually encourages the absorption of capasaicin and beer can make a fiery bowl of chili seem even hotter. A better choice would be a glass of milk, which fights the fire, as do all dairy products, which explains why combination plates in most Tex-Mex restaurants, as well as many recipes, add a dollop of sour cream as a garnish. But if a glass of milk has a negative effect on an urban cowboy's image, starchy food can also

Above: this illustration from 1874 shows a woman kneading tortillas in archetypal Mexican surroundings. A writer who visited the area at the time described the women as "ceaselessly rolling out the tortilla, or frying it on the iron plate that sits over their bit of a fire."

neutralize the heat. Rice is a perfect choice, as any fan of fiery Szechuan Chinese food can tell you, but some crusty bread or even crackers can calm down any Tex-Mex dish, even one that would otherwise fog your glasses.

In many recipes, there is no substitute for fresh chiles, but if capasaicin can do strange things to your taste buds, it is also capable of burning your skin and calls for care in handling. Rubber gloves are always recommended while cutting away the seeds and veins, and special care should be taken not to touch your face and especially your eyes while handling the pods. And even though the rubber gloves have protected them, your hands should be thoroughly washed with hot soapy water after the job is done.

Dried chiles are useful in many Tex-Mex recipes because their flavors are more concentrated. If the pods aren't broken, they can be stored in covered containers for as long as six months, but before they are used, they need to be brought back to life. To do that, simply dry-roast them in a skillet or in the oven for two or three minutes and then to cover them with

very hot, but not boiling, water for about twenty minutes more.

Like tomatoes and corn, the world knew nothing of chiles before the Spanish arrived in the Americas, but there is hardly a corner of the world where they aren't found today. Indeed, some cuisines are so centered on them, it is hard to imagine what people did for fun in the kitchen and dining room before the end of the 15th century. But there is another staple that Texas cooks have used for generations to add a special flavor to their barbecues and other grilled dishes that was largely a secret ingredient until a decade or so ago when restaurateurs around the country began raising the level of border food to heights that had previously been restricted to the Southwest.

In some ways, it's strange the secret had been kept for so long. The Greeks had a word for it, "prosopis," and in fact, botanists still call it that. The Aztecs, who used it liberally, called it "mizquitl," which is the source of the modern American name, mesquite, the special wood whose smoke not only enhances the natural flavors of grilled food, but adds a subtle sweet flavor of its own not possible with any other kind of wood.

The mesquite tree is a perfect example of one of nature's creations that on first glance seems to have no other purpose than to harrass man and beast, but turns out to be a great gift of nature once its orneriness is overlooked. In Texas, where it is known as switch mesquite, it is more bush than tree and it ranks among the ugliest denizens of the desert country. Its trunk is gnarled, its bark scaly, its branches twisted like a nest of serpents. The mesquite's leaves are feathery and might be called attractive, and even inviting on a hot summer day when they provide the only shade available, until you realize that they serve to camouflage the thorns underneath, some of which are as much as two inches long and all of them sharp as needles. It is the mortal enemy of other plants that share its space because even though it thrives in dry country, mesquite is one of the thirstiest plants alive. It isn't unusual for its main root to grow downward as far as two hundred feet in search of water and for the rest of its root system to radiate outward for sixty or seventy feet sucking every drop of moisture in its path. It is also one of the fastest-spreading of all trees and once established, the hardest of all to eliminate.

Cut down a mesquite tree and the roots will send up a couple of new shoots to replace it. And any rancher with money enough to dig up the roots finds it only a temporary solution because cattle consider mesquite seeds a kind of delicacy and because they are indigestable, the steers do a fine job of planting new trees. And to add insult to injury, in dry seasons when grass withers, the mesquite produces more seed pods than in times when the grasses are lush, making them all the more attractive to hungry critters.

The wood was valuable to the early settlers in the Southwest for making fence posts, animal pens and small shelters but cowhands, who sneered at such things, found it perfect for cooking. Almost no other hardwood burns with a hotter flame and it ignites easily without any tinder, which is a boon for modern outdoor cooks who don't believe the fumes of petroleum-based lighter fuels add a thing to the flavor of their barbecue. Because mesquite coals are so much hotter, they sear food quickly and lock in the natural juices, and because the heat is longer-lasting, food is cooked more evenly. But the real advantage is mesquite's aroma, which enhances the flavor of beef as well as pork and game. In fact, just about anything cooked Tex-Mex style is better if it has been cooked over a mesquite fire.

Among those who would have said Amen to that statement were the cowboys who led the great cattle drives northward from Texas in the years after the Civil War, or at least the men who drove the chuckwagons. Those cooks, always the most important man in any outfit after the trail boss himself, were probably the first to export border cooking north of the Red River and their lives weren't worth a thing if they didn't get it right. Among their duties was to move far ahead of the herd to select a perfect spot to make camp for the night, which meant that they were the first to run into trouble if there was any up ahead. But no matter what it took, they had to locate a campsite before the line of steers showed up on the horizon. It had to have water, of course, but more important was a stand of mesquite so they could get a hot fire going fast because as soon as the cattle were settled down, it would be time to eat, and no excuses were ever accepted. It was especially important when they got up at the crack of dawn to get the coffee made and to get the sourdough biscuits cooked. The latter were made in a dutch oven from starter the cook prepared before they left Texas by

Above: an early photograph of two chefs from Waco, Texas.

mixing flour and salt together with water and storing it in a covered cask. It has to be kept warm all the way to Kansas, but if it couldn't be allowed to get chilled, it was also destroyed if it got too hot and either disaster was always lurking out there on the prairie. Although cowboys thrived on beef and beans, any cook who lost his stash of sourdough starter could probably expect to be forced to hit the trail on his own. Making the biscuits wasn't all that hard, all that was required was to put a bit of starter in the center of the greased dutch oven, add some flour, salt, warm water and soda and then knead it until it felt just right. After that, all that was left to do was to put the dutch oven on the hot coals for a half hour or so, and add more flour, salt and warm water to the starter mixture in anticipation of the next day's breakfast. It was a simple process, but if the biscuits weren't perfect, it could not only ruin a cowpoke's day, but would guarantee a rough ride for the cook. Fortunately for many of them, their insistence on mesquite fires saved the hides of most of them. No wonder a good cook was paid $100 a month. He earned every penny. On the other hand, it should be noted that the average cowboy didn't believe that mesquite smoke did much to the trailside cuisine, and if they couldn't think of anything else to gripe about, the smoke could get them started. They had good reason to scorn the thorny bushes that their steers were forever wandering into, but they were usually too exhausted to notice any subtlety in their grub anyway. The bill of fare on a cattle drive consisted mostly of cooked pinto beans, coffee and those inevitable biscuits. Once in a while the monotony was broken with a pan fried steak or a bowl of "son-of-a-bitch stew," made from the intestines of nursing calves. The routine didn't vary at all for the three months it usually took to drive a herd from Texas up to Kansas and once the job was over and the cowboys were finished letting off a little steam, all they wanted was to get back to Texas and some of that good old down-home cooking.

During the years of the great cattle drives, the men who earned their living at it usually spent the off-season working at odd jobs, bragging about their exploits during the previous summer and arguing a lot among themselves. And chances are the thing they argued most about was what constituted a perfect bowl of chili. Many Texans still do.

Just as many of them argue over whether it is barbecue or chili that is the favorite food of the Lone Star State and even after the State Legislature came down on the side of chili by voting it the state's official dish, the debate is still as fierce as ever. The barbecue partisans say their favorite dish should have won because the chiliheads can't even agree among themselves about how to make a perfect bowl of red. But in their official protest at the State House in Austin, they did admit it was so simple to make a pot of chili that even little children could do it. "The hardest thing about making chili," they said, "is finding somebody to eat it."

It was hitting below the belt, to be sure, and it wasn't long before the other camp countered the charge with figures to prove that chili is to Texas what the potato was to the Irish, what pasta is to the Italians and rice is to the Chinese. Nearly everyone involved had what they characterized as the perfect recipe for real Texas-style chili, but as their neighbors on the barbecue side of the debate had pointed out in the first place, they couldn't agree about what was real and what wasn't.

The ensuing war led to a World Championship Chili Cookoff at Terlinga, Texas, in 1966 and probably because it ended in a draw, it has become an annual event. And all over Texas these days, regional events are held to pick local champs to go on the the big one at Terlinga. Showmanship counts, of course, in the end cooking a pot of chili is a serious business among the contestants. They get attention with such untraditional ingredients as rattlesnake meat, raccoon or armadillo and some even substitute chicken for meat. About the only thing they all agree on is that it is a sacrilege to add beans to anything described as chili. Beyond that, it seems, anything goes. The day-long festivities include more than just cooking. They are marked with heavy-duty beer-drinking competitions, wet T-shirt contests, Wild West-style shootouts and some of the contests remembered from Sunday school picnics like egg-tossing, one-legged races and lemon rolls. But cooks with serious intentions of going on to Terlinga know that the basic rule of a good pot of chili is to keep it simple. Most of the winning recipes have a thing or two in common: cubes of beef that have been marinated and browned, then seasoned with such things as coriander, cumin, garlic, oregano, paprika and crushed chiles. They almost never contain onions, tomatoes or bell peppers and never, ever, beans. The binding ingredient is masa harina, a dough made from ground dried corn. The rest is whatever the cook decides it takes to make a perfect bowl of red. And as in all Tex-Mex cooking it is a combination of imagination and tender loving care.

But Tex-Mex food, as you are about to discover for yourself, is more than a memorable barbecue or a perfect bowl of red. Its hallmark is a studied lack of pretense, and although modern Texans are comfortable in Continental-style restaurants, they are at their most contented when the accent is homey. They've tasted caviar, but prefer pickled black-eyed peas. They've dined on swordfish steak, but would be just as happy with a mess of fried catfish. They are as willing to try new ideas as any other Americans, but in the end, the ones that stay with them are the ones that fit best with the ideas of their ancestors. It is why the flavor of Texas isn't likely to change any time soon. And why so much of the rest of the country is running to catch up.

CHAPTER ONE
Soups and Appetizers

Above: the ghost town of Terlingua was once a city of over 2,000 which sprang up following the discovery of mercury in 1890.

*T*he varied cuisine that comes together under the banner of Tex-Mex cooking is succinctly reflected in the variety of its soups and appetizers. The traditional ingredients of Southwestern cooking – beef, chiles, corn, avocados – recur in many dishes, but in a variety of combinations. One of the most popular appetizers is, of course, guacamole, but not to be missed are the many delicious, hearty soups. These reflect the cowboy's love of filling dishes and the enduring popularity of soups south of the border. Delicious, heart-warming soups are ubiquitious in Mexico and feature a variety of ingredients, from beef or pork with onion and garlic and a puree of tomatoes, to zesty seafood chowders flavored with lime. Thankfully, more and more of these soups are finding their way across the border to add extra spice to many a restaurant menu.

Cornmeal Pancakes

Cornmeal, either yellow, white or blue, is an important ingredient in Tex-Mex recipes. Here it's combined with corn to make a light appetizer, or the pancakes can be served as a side dish to a main course.

1 cup yellow cornmeal
1 Tbsp flour
1 tsp baking soda
1 tsp salt
2 eggs, separated
2 cups buttermilk
Oil
10 oz frozen corn
Sour cream
Red pepper preserves
Green onions, chopped

Sift the dry ingredients into a bowl, adding any coarse meal that remains in the strainer. Mix the egg yolks and buttermilk together and gradually beat into the dry ingredients. Cover and leave to stand for at least 15 minutes. Whisk the egg whites until stiff, but not dry, and fold into the cornmeal mixture. Lightly grease a skillet with oil and drop in about 2 tablespoons of batter. Sprinkle with the corn and allow to cook until the underside is golden brown. Turn the pancakes

Chile Vegetable Soup

Chiles and lime juice give this soup the startling sharp flavors so typical of Tex-Mex cooking.

1 Tbsp oil
1 onion, chopped
4 oz canned whole green chiles, quartered
4 cups chicken stock
1 large potato, peeled and cut into short strips
Full quantity Taco Sauce recipe (see page 30)
1 Tbsp lime juice
Salt
Tortilla chips and lime slices, to garnish

Heat the oil in a large saucepan and sauté the onion until translucent. Add the green chiles, stock, potato, and taco sauce. Cover the pan and simmer soup for 20 minutes. Stir in the lime juice and add salt. Serve in individual bowls with tortilla chips. Cut a thin slice of lime to float in each bowl of soup. Serves 4.

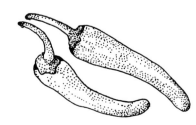

and cook the second side until golden. Continue with the remaining batter and corn. Keep the cooked pancakes warm. To serve, place three pancakes on warm side plates. Add a spoonful of sour cream and red pepper preserves to each and sprinkle with finely sliced or shredded green onions. Serves 4.

Above left: the cowboy's basic diet has altered surprisingly little in the last century; it is the hearty combination of beans, meat, biscuits and coffee that still provide sustenance.

Beef & Bean Soup

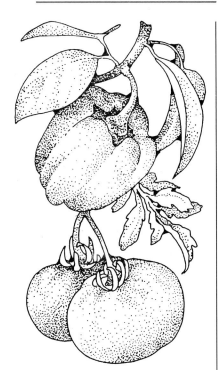

The use of the Tex-Mex specialty of refried beans in this recipe has the dual purpose of adding local flavor and thickening this hearty soup. Cumin, cinnamon, and cayenne are all strong components of the Tex-Mex character.

1 large onion, finely chopped
1 red bell pepper, finely chopped
2 stalks celery, chopped
2 Tbsps oil
8 oz ground beef
6 tomatoes, peeled, seeded and chopped
15 oz canned refried beans
1 tsp ground cumin
1 tsp chile powder
Pinch of cinnamon and cayenne pepper
1 tsp garlic powder or paste
Salt and pepper
2 cups beef stock

Fry the onion, bell pepper, and celery in the oil in a large saucepan until softened. Add the beef and fry over medium heat until well browned. Add the tomatoes and refried beans with the spices, garlic, and seasoning and mix well. Stir in the stock and bring to a boil. Cover and simmer gently for 30 minutes, stirring occasionally. Pour the soup into a blender or food processor and purée. The soup will be quite thick and not completely smooth. Adjust the seasoning and serve with tortilla chips. Top with sour cream if desired. Serves 4.

Shrimp Acapulco

These shrimp laced with Tex-Mex spices make an exciting appetizer, or if the bread is cut smaller they can be served with cocktails.

4 slices bread, crusts removed
6 Tbsps softened butter
6 oz cooked and peeled shrimp
½ tsp chile powder
¼ tsp paprika
¼ tsp cumin
Salt and pepper
Watercress, to garnish

Cut the bread slices in half and spread with 2 tablespoons of the butter. Butter both sides sparingly. Place the bread on a cookie sheet and cook in a preheated 350° F oven for 10-15 minutes until golden brown. Keep warm. Melt the remaining butter in a small pan and add the shrimp, spices, and seasoning and stir well. Heat through completely and spoon on top of the bread slices. Garnish with watercress and serve hot. Serves 4.

Above left: this early photograph shows a family preparing to take their produce to market.

Guacamole

It is essential for the Tex-Mex cook to have guacamole in his or her repertoire. It is commonly served as a dip with tortilla chips; it is served as a side-dish to be eaten with barbecued meats and chilis; and it is piled onto and into many of those wrapped-up Tex-Mex specialties such as flautas, chimichangas and enchiladas.

1 medium onion, finely chopped
1 clove garlic, minced
Grated rind and juice of ½ lime
½ quantity Taco Sauce recipe (see page 30)
3 large avocados
Pinch of salt
1 Tbsp chopped fresh coriander
Coriander leaves, to garnish

Mix the onion, garlic, rind and juice of lime, and the taco sauce together in a large mixing bowl. Cut the avocados in half lengthwise. Twist the halves gently in opposite directions to separate. Hit the stone with a large, sharp knife and twist the embedded knife to remove the stone. Place the avocado halves cut side down on a chopping board. Lightly score the skin lengthwise and gently pull back to peel. Alternatively, scoop out avocado flesh with a spoon, scraping the skin well. Chop the avocado roughly and immediately place in the bowl with the onion and lime. Use a potato masher to break up the avocado until almost smooth. Do not over-mash. Season with salt and stir in the chopped coriander. Spoon into a serving bowl and garnish with coriander leaves. Serves 8 as a dip.

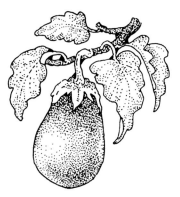

Above right: Palo Duro Canyon in Texas has been carved over millions of years by the flow of the Red River and the erosive action of wind and rain. Below: the old Spanish church of Mission San José, San Antonio.

CHAPTER TWO
Tortillas and Turnovers

Above: a 19th-century engraving shows Mexican women preparing tortillas in the traditional manner.

A favorite part of many Tex-Mex meals are the myriad varieties of delicious stuffed tortillas. Packed with anything from spicy ground beef to vegetables and refried beans, these mouthwatering parcels of Tex-Mex flavor owe much to the street food of Mexico. Here, tortillas are wrapped around a filling and sold on the streets and in the markets as a convenient ready-to-eat snack. Tex-Mex versions tend to be larger and a little less easy to eat than their Mexican counterparts, but they taste just as divine. The great attraction of filled tortillas is their adaptability; almost any ingredient can be used as a filling and combined with sauces, toppings, and salads to give a dish that is as individual as its creator!

Tortillas

Flautas

Flautas, literally flutes, are rather elegant double length stuffed tortillas, made by filling and rolling two overlapping tortillas at once. Tex-Mex style would be to eat them with rice, refried beans and a tomato and avocado salad.

1 Tbsp oil
8 oz chicken, skinned, boned and ground or finely chopped
1 small onion, finely chopped
½ green bell pepper, finely chopped
½-1 chile, seeded and finely chopped
3 oz frozen corn
6 black olives, pitted and chopped
½ cup heavy cream
Salt
12 prepared tortillas (see page 26)
Taco sauce (see page 30), guacamole, and sour cream for toppings

Heat the oil in a medium skillet and add the chicken, onion, and bell pepper. Cook over moderate heat, stirring frequently to break up the pieces of chicken. When the chicken is cooked and the vegetables are softened, add the chile, corn, olives, cream, and salt. Bring to a boil and boil rapidly,

Borrowed from Mexico, these have become indispensible in Tex-Mex cooking and are used as a base for tacos, enchiladas and other Tex-Mex dishes. In Mexico the tortilla is made from lime-soaked dried corn, which is wetted and ground into a dough called masa. Here, wheat flour is used.

2 cups all-purpose flour (more if necessary)
2 tsps baking powder
Pinch of salt
4 Tbsps vegetable shortening
½-¾ cup hot water
Oil for frying

Sift the flour, baking powder and salt into a bowl. Cut in the vegetable shortening until the mixture resembles coarse crumbs. Add water, mixing until absorbed. Knead gently and add more flour if the dough is too sticky. Cover and leave to rest for 15 minutes. Divide the dough into ten even-sized pieces. Roll into balls on a floured surface, cover and leave to stand for 20 minutes. Roll out each ball on a lightly floured surface to a circle 7 inches in diameter. Cover the finished tortillas while rolling all the remaining dough. Place a lightly oiled skillet over high heat. Fry the tortillas individually on both sides until bubbles form on the surface. Stack them as they are cooked and set them aside until ready to use. Makes 12.

stirring continuously, to reduce and thicken the cream. Place 2 tortillas side by side on a clean work surface, overlapping them by about 2 inches. Spoon some of the chicken mixture in a line across the middle of the 2 tortillas, roll up the 2 together and secure with wooden picks. Fry each flauta in about ½ -inch oil in a large sauté pan. Do not allow them to get very brown. Drain on paper towels. Arrange flautas on serving plates and top with sour cream, guacamole and taco sauce. Serves 6.

Right: this fascinating photograph, dating from 1904, shows children enjoying making tortillas with their maid. Above left: The Ranching Heritage Center in Lubbock contains a variety of relocated and restored ranching structures.

Tacos

This is one of the classic mainstays of Tex-Mex cooking which always looks impressive when served at home and is easily made with packaged taco shells. A good tip is to place the empty taco shells on their open ends when warming to keep them from closing up, so making filling easier.

12 taco shells

BEEF FILLING
1 Tbsp oil
1 pound ground beef
1 medium onion, chopped
2 tsps ground cumin
1 clove garlic, minced
2 tsps chile powder
Pinch of paprika
Salt and pepper

TOPPINGS
Shredded lettuce
Shredded cheese
Tomatoes, seeded and chopped
Chopped green onions
Avocado slices
Sour cream
Jalapeno peppers
Taco Sauce (see page 30)

CHICKEN FILLING
3 Tbsps butter or margarine
1 medium onion, chopped
1 small red bell pepper, chopped
2 Tbsps sliced almonds
12 oz chicken breasts, skinned and finely chopped
Salt and pepper
1 piece fresh ginger root, peeled and chopped
6 Tbsps milk
2 tsps cornstarch
½ cup sour cream

Heat oil for beef filling in a large skillet and brown the beef and onion, breaking the meat up with a fork as it cooks. Add spices, garlic, and seasoning and cook about 20 minutes. Set aside.

For the chicken filling, melt 2 tablespoons butter or margarine in a medium saucepan and add the onion. Cook slowly until softened. Add the bell pepper and almonds and cook slowly until the almonds are lightly browned. Stir often during cooking. Remove to a plate and set aside. Melt the remaining butter in the same saucepan and cook the chicken for about 5 minutes, turning frequently. Season and return the onion mixture to the pan along with the chopped ginger. Blend milk and cornstarch and stir into the chicken mixture. Bring to a boil and stir until very thick. Mix in the sour cream and cook gently to heat through. Do not boil.

Heat the taco shells on a cookie sheet in a preheated 350° F oven for 2-3 minutes. Place on the sheet with the open ends down. To fill, hold the shell in one hand, and spoon in about 1 tablespoon of either beef or chicken filling. Next, add a layer of shredded lettuce, followed by a layer of shredded cheese. Add choice of other toppings and finally spoon on some taco sauce. Serves 6.

Above: rounding up the horses on a Texan ranch. Although there are fewer cowboys in Texas these days, they still run their longhorns through Texas' wide open spaces.

Taco Sauce

This basic recipe has many uses in Tex-Mex cooking. Use as a sauce or topping for fish, meat or poultry main dishes. Use in tacos, tostadas, nachos and as a dip for tortilla chips or vegetable crudités.

1 Tbsp oil
1 onion, diced
1 green bell pepper, diced
½-1 red or green chile
½ tsp ground cumin
½ tsp ground coriander
½ clove garlic, minced
Pinch of salt, pepper and sugar
14 oz canned tomatoes
Tomato paste (optional)

Heat the oil in a heavy-based saucepan and when hot, add the onion and bell pepper. Cook slowly to soften slightly. Chop the chile and add with the cumin, coriander, garlic and cook a further 2-3 minutes. Add sugar, seasonings, and tomatoes with their juice. Break up the tomatoes with a fork or a potato masher. Cook a further 5-6 minutes over moderate heat to reduce and thicken slightly. Add tomato paste for color, if necessary. Adjust seasoning and use hot or cold according to your recipe. Makes ½ pint.

Gulf Coast Tacos

Around the Gulf of Mexico, ever popular Tex-Mex tacos take on a local taste with a seafood filling.

6 Tortillas (see page 26)
Oil for frying

GREEN CHILI SALSA
1 Tbsp oil
3 Tomatillos, husks removed
1 clove garlic
1 oz coriander leaves
2 green chiles
Juice of 1 lime
½ cup sour cream
Pinch of salt and sugar

FILLING INGREDIENTS
8 oz large raw shrimp, peeled
8 oz raw scallops, quartered if large
1 tsp coriander seed, crushed
1 shallot, finely chopped
Salt and pepper
6 Tbsps white wine
1 small jicama root, peeled and cut into thin matchstick strips
Coriander leaves and lime wedges

Prepare the Tortillas according to the recipe. Heat the oil for the salsa in a small skillet and slice the tomatillos. Sauté them for about 3 minutes to soften. Place in a food processor along with the garlic, coriander, chiles, and lime juice. Purée until smooth. Fold in the sour cream, adjust seasoning and chill. Heat oil in a deep sauté pan to a depth of at least 2 inches. When hot, place in a tortilla and press down under the oil with a metal spoon. When the tortilla starts to puff up, take it out and immediately fold in half to form a shell. Hold in shape until it cools slightly and sets. Repeat with the remaining tortillas. Keep them warm in an oven, standing on their open ends. This prevents them from closing.

Place the shrimp, scallops, coriander seeds, shallot, and salt and pepper in a sauté pan with the wine and water to barely cover. Cook for about 8 minutes, stirring occasionally. The shrimp should turn pink and the scallops will look opaque when cooked. Fill the taco shells with the jicama. Remove the seafood from the liquid with a draining spoon and arrange on top of the jicama. Top with the salsa and garnish with coriander leaves. Serve with lime wedges. Serves 6.

Above left: preparing a meal outside a Mexican jacal – a traditional but made of wooden planks and straw or rushes.

30

Enchiladas

Sauces and fillings for enchiladas, a Mexican specialty brought into the Tex-Mex fold, can be infinitely varied to suit individual tastes.

12 prepared tortillas (see page 26)
4 Tbsps shredded cheese
Sliced green onions, to garnish

SAUCE
10 ripe tomatoes, peeled, seeded and chopped
1 small onion, chopped
1-2 Tbsps tomato paste
1-2 green or red chiles, seeded and chopped
1 clove garlic, minced
Salt
Pinch of sugar
2 Tbsps butter or margarine
2 eggs
1 cup heavy cream

MEAT FILLING
12 oz ground pork
1 small red bell pepper, chopped
4 Tbsps raisins
4 Tbsps pine nuts
Salt and pepper

To make sauce, place tomatoes, onion, tomato paste, chiles, garlic, salt, and sugar in a blender or food processor and purée until smooth. Melt butter or margarine in a large saucepan. Add the paste and simmer for 5 minutes. Beat together the eggs and cream, mixing well. Add a spoonful of the hot tomato paste to the cream and eggs and mix quickly. Return mixture to the saucepan with the rest of the tomato paste. Heat slowly, stirring constantly, until the mixture thickens. Do not boil.

Meanwhile, cook the pork and bell pepper slowly in a large skillet. Use a fork to break up the meat as it cooks. Turn up the heat when the pork is nearly cooked and fry briskly for a few minutes. Add the raisins, pine nuts, and seasoning. Combine about ¼ of the sauce with the meat and divide mixture evenly among all the tortillas. Spoon on the filling to one side of the center and roll up the tortilla around it, leaving the ends open and some of the filling showing. Place enchiladas seam side down in a baking dish and pour over the remaining sauce, leaving the ends uncovered. Sprinkle over the cheese and bake in a preheated 350° F oven for 15-20 minutes, or until the sauce begins to bubble. Sprinkle with the sliced onions and serve immediately. Serves 6.

Above: the state flower of Texas, the bluebonnet. There are more than 5,000 different kinds of flower in the Lone Star State, but the bluebonnet is among the most beautiful.

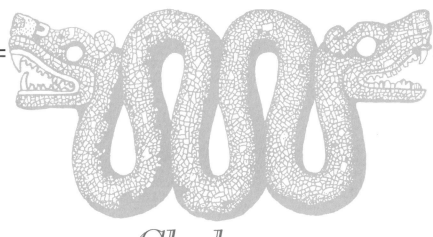

Chalupas

These are tortillas in another form, this time a snack with spicy meat. For a main course, add Refried Beans or Spicy Rice and Beans as an accompaniment.

½ quantity Tortilla recipe (see page 26)
Oil, for frying
Full quantity Red Sauce (see recipe for Southwestern Stir-fry, page 52)
12 oz ground beef
2 cloves garlic, minced
1 tsp dried oregano
2 tsps cumin
Salt and pepper
3 oz frozen corn
4 Tbsps raisins

TOPPINGS
6-8 green onions, chopped
4-6 tomatoes, diced
½ a small head lettuce, shredded
½ cup sour cream
1 cup shredded cheese

Prepare the tortillas according to the recipe and divide the dough in 10. After the required resting time, roll the balls of dough into 3½-inch rounds. Prepare the red sauce according to the recipe instructions and set it aside. Heat at least 2 inches of oil in a skillet, sauté pan or medium saucepan. When hot, place in one tortilla at a time and fry briefly until just crisp. Drain and keep them warm. Cook the beef slowly in a large skillet until the fat begins to render. Add the garlic, oregano, and cumin and raise the heat to brown the meat. Season to taste and then stir in enough of the red sauce to moisten the meat well. Add the corn and raisins, cover the pan and leave to stand for 5 minutes. Spoon the meat onto the tortillas and drizzle over more sauce. Garnish with your choice of toppings.

Chimichangas

Chimichangas are delicious deep-fried tortilla parcels containing chili, onions, and cheese. A Tex-Mex meal would feature them as an appetizer or a main course served with rice and refried beans.

6 flour tortillas (see page 26)
½ quantity Chili con Carne recipe (see page 54)
6 lettuce leaves, shredded
6 green onions, chopped
3 oz cheddar cheese, shredded
Oil for frying
½ quantity Guacamole recipe (see page 22)
½ cup sour cream
1 tomato, seeded and chopped

Wrap the tortillas in foil and place in a warm oven for 5 minutes to make them pliable. Heat the chili briefly and spoon about 2 tablespoons onto the center of each tortilla. Top with lettuce, onions and cheese. Fold in the sides to make a parcel, making sure all the filling is enclosed. Heat about 1 inch of oil in a large sauté pan and when hot lower in the chimichangas, folded side down first. Cook 2-4 at a time depending on the size of the pan. Cook for 3

minutes and carefully turn over. Cook a further 3 minutes and remove to paper towels and drain. Repeat with remaining chimichangas. Spoon the guacamole over the top of each and drizzle over the sour cream. Sprinkle over the chopped tomato and serve immediately. Serves 6 as an appetizer, or 3 as a main course.

Above: an illustration from 1878 of Mexican women making frijoles in a rural kitchen in the Tierras Calientes.

Burritos

The name is Spanish for "little donkeys" and the dish is a very popular one. Beans are the traditional filling, but meat may be used as well. Burritos can be served as an appetizer or as a main course with rice and guacamole.

6 flour tortillas (see page 26)
1 onion, chopped
1 Tbsp oil
1 pound canned refried beans
6 lettuce leaves, shredded
4 oz cheddar cheese, shredded
2 tomatoes, sliced
2 Tbsps snipped chives
Full quantity Taco Sauce recipe (see page 30)
½ cup sour cream
Chopped coriander leaves

Wrap tortillas in foil and heat in a warm oven to soften. Cook the onion in the oil until soft but not colored. Add the beans and heat through. Spoon the mixture down the center of each tortilla. Top with lettuce, cheese, tomatoes, and chives. Fold over the sides to form long rectangular parcel. Make sure the filling is completely enclosed. Place burritos in an ovenproof dish, cover and cook in a preheated 350° F oven for about 20 minutes. Spoon over the taco sauce. Top with sour cream and sprinkle with chopped coriander to serve. Serves 6 as an appetizer.

Empanadas

This is a Tex-Mex recipe that has been adapted from the Spanish pastries popular in Mexico.

Triple quantity pastry recipe from Chile Shrimp Quiche (see page 46)
1 egg

FILLING
1 onion, chopped
1 clove garlic, finely chopped
1 small green bell pepper, chopped
1 Tbsp oil
8 oz ground beef
1 tsp unsweetened cocoa
1 Tbsp flour
½ tsp ground cumin
½ tsp paprika
½ tsp dried oregano, crushed
Salt and pepper
1-2 chiles, seeded and chopped
2 Tbsps tomato paste
3 Tbsps water
2 Tbsps sliced almonds
2 Tbsps raisins

Prepare the pastry according to the recipe for Chile Shrimp Quiche. Cook the onion, garlic, and bell pepper in the oil in a skillet until soft but not colored. Add the meat and fry quickly until well browned. Add the cocoa, flour, spices, oregano, and seasonings. Stir well and cook briefly before adding the chiles, tomato paste, and water. Cook slowly for 10-15 minutes. Add nuts and raisins and allow to cool. Roll out the pastry on a floured surface and cut out 6 rounds using a 6-inch plate as a guide. Place the cooled filling on one side of the rounds of pastry and dampen the edges with water. Fold over and press to seal the edges. Crimp the edges if desired. Place on cookie sheets and brush with a mixture of beaten egg and salt. Make sure the egg glaze is brushed on evenly. Prick once or twice with a fork and bake in a 425° F oven for about 15 minutes, or until golden brown. Makes 6.

Above left: the ranch cook, who has the unenviable and seemingly endless task of keeping the ranch hands fed.

CHAPTER THREE
Fish and Seafood

Above: comancheros in Josie's Gaslight Square, Corpus Christi.

*T*he influence of Mexico's fishing tradition, and the growth of interest in healthful eating has heralded a welcome growth in the popularity of Tex-Mex seafood dishes. The Gulf waters provide an abundance of fresh delights, from sparkling shrimp to red snapper and swordfish, while the area's rivers provide such favorites as bass, trout, and catfish. A wonderfully adaptable ingredient, fish and seafood is served up in numerous exciting ways. Shrimp is combined with a spicy taco sauce, while freshwater fish is often coated in a spicy cornmeal and served with lime wedges. Undoubtedly, Tex-Mex cuisine owes a great debt of gratitude to the native Americans who showed the way in utilizing local produce, from local brook trout to the ubiquitous corn, to create a regional cuisine that is uniquely diverse.

Shrimp Veracruz

Veracruz is a port on the Gulf of Mexico which lends its name to this colorful seafood Tex-Mex dish.

1 Tbsp oil
1 onion, chopped
1 large green bell pepper, cut into 1½-inch strips
2-3 green chiles, seeded and chopped
Double quantity Taco Sauce recipe (see page 30)
2 tomatoes, peeled and roughly chopped
12 pimiento-stuffed olives, halved
2 tsps capers
¼ tsp ground cumin
Salt
1 pound shrimp, uncooked
Juice of 1 lime

Heat the oil in a large skillet and add the onion and bell pepper. Cook until soft but not colored. Add chiles, taco sauce, tomatoes, olives, capers, cumin, and salt. Bring to a boil and then lower the heat to simmer for 5 minutes. Remove black veins, if present, from the rounded side of the shrimp with a wooden pick. Add the shrimp to the sauce and cook until they curl up and turn pink and opaque. Add the lime juice to taste and serve. Serves 6.

Swordfish with Grapefruit Tequila Salsa

Swordfish from the Gulf of Mexico spiked with the tart flavors of local citrus fruits and tequila – the liquor distilled from the Peyote cactus – makes a true Tex-Mex delicacy. For extra flavor, and to enrich the fish, the swordfish steaks may be marinated in a lime juice and oil mixture for up to an hour beforehand.

4-6 ruby or pink grapefruit (depending on size)
1 lime
½ green chile, seeded and finely diced
1 green onion, finely chopped
2 Tbsps chopped fresh coriander
1 Tbsp sugar
3 Tbsps tequila
Juice of 1 lime
2 Tbsps oil
Black pepper, to taste
4-8 swordfish steaks (depending on size)
Coriander sprigs for garnish

Remove the zest from the grapefruit and lime with a zester and set it aside. Remove all the pith from the

grapefruit and segment them. Squeeze the lime for juice. Mix the grapefruit and citrus zests with the chile, onion, coriander, sugar, tequila, and lime juice and set aside. Mix remaining lime juice, oil, and pepper together and brush both sides of the fish. Place under a pre-heated broiler and cook for about 4 minutes each side depending on distance from the heat source. To serve, place a coriander sprig on each fish steak and serve with the grapefruit salsa. Serves 4.

Above left: Harrell House in Lubbock's Ranching Heritage Center is the perfect example of a ranch home at the end of the nineteenth century.

Plaice with Spicy Tomato Sauce

With Mexico and Texas both bordering the Gulf of Mexico it's logical that Tex-Mex cooking should incorporate fish into its repertoire – and not just the famous barbecues and chilis. This is good served with rice and an avocado salad.

3 oz cream cheese
1 tsp dried oregano
Pinch cayenne pepper
4 whole fillets of plaice
Lime slices and dill, to garnish

TOMATO SAUCE
1 Tbsp oil
1 small onion, chopped
1 stalk celery, chopped
1 chile, seeded and chopped
¼ tsp each ground cumin, coriander and ginger
½ red and ½ green bell pepper, chopped
14 oz canned tomatoes
1 Tbsp tomato paste
Salt, pepper, and a pinch sugar

To prepare the sauce heat the oil in a heavy-based pan and cook the onion, celery, chile, and spices for about 5 minutes over very low heat. Add the bell peppers and the remaining sauce ingredients and bring to a boil. Reduce heat and simmer 15-20 minutes, stirring occasionally. Set aside while preparing the fish. Mix the cream cheese, oregano, and cayenne pepper together and set aside. Skin the fillets using a filleting knife. Start at the tail end and hold the knife at a slight angle to the skin. Push the knife along using a sawing motion, with the blade against the skin. Dip fingers in salt to make it easier to hold onto the fish skin. Gradually separate the fish from the skin. Spread the cheese filling on all 4 fillets and roll each up. Secure with wooden picks. Place the fillets in a lightly greased baking dish, cover and cook for 10 minutes in a preheated 350° F oven. Pour over the tomato sauce and cook a further 10-15 minutes. Fish is cooked when it feels firm and looks opaque. Garnish with lime slices and dill. Serves 4.

Above: the mountains of Big Bend National Park.
Left: a shrimp boat, in the Port of Galveston.

42

Fried Bass in Cornmeal

Corn, the staple of the aboriginal peoples of the USA and Mexico, was adopted by the New World settlers. It continues to be the mainstay of Tex-Mex cooking, not only as the basis of tortilla dough but also as a crisp and subtly-flavored coating for fried foods. For extra Tex-Mex taste serve this bass with red chile preserves or relish.

2 cups yellow cornmeal
2 Tbsps flour
Pinch of salt
2 tsps cayenne pepper
1 tsp ground cumin
2 tsps garlic granules
2 pounds freshwater bass or other whitefish fillets
Milk
Oil for deep frying
Lime wedges, to garnish

Mix the cornmeal, flour, salt, cayenne, cumin, and garlic together in a shallow container or on a piece of wax paper. Skin the fillets if desired. Dip them into the milk and then lift to allow the excess to drip off. Place the fish in the cornmeal mixture and turn with two forks or, if using paper, lift the ends and toss the fish to coat. Meanwhile, heat oil in a deep frying pan, large saucepan or deep-fat fryer. Add the fish in small batches and cook until the fillets float to the surface. Turn over and cook to brown lightly and evenly. Drain on paper towels and serve immediately with lime wedges. Serves 4.

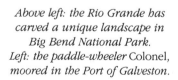

Above left: the Rio Grande has carved a unique landscape in Big Bend National Park.
Left: the paddle-wheeler Colonel, *moored in the Port of Galveston.*

Chile Shrimp Quiche

Chiles, green onions and garlic give this shrimp quiche Tex-Mex bite and flavor.

PASTRY
1 cup all-purpose flour
2 Tbsps butter or margarine
2 Tbsps vegetable shortening
2-4 Tbsps cold water

FILLING
4 eggs
½ cup milk
½ cup light cream
½ clove garlic, minced
Salt
1 cup cheddar cheese, shredded
3 green onions, chopped
2 green chiles, seeded and chopped
8 oz cooked and peeled shrimp
Salt
Cooked, unpeeled shrimp and parsley sprigs for garnish

Sift the flour with a pinch of salt into a mixing bowl, or place in a food processor and mix once or twice. Cut in the butter and shortening until the mixture resembles fine bread crumbs, or work in the food processor, being careful not to over-mix. Mix in the liquid gradually, adding enough to bring the dough together in a ball. In a food processor, add the liquid through the funnel while the machine is running. Wrap the dough well and chill for 20-30 minutes.

Roll out the dough on a well-floured surface with a floured rolling pin. Wrap the circle of dough around the rolling pin to lift it into a 10-inch pie pan. Unroll the dough over the pan. Carefully press the dough onto the bottom and up the sides of the pan, taking care not to stretch it. Roll the rolling pin over the top of the pan to remove excess dough, or cut off with a sharp knife.

Mix the eggs, milk, cream, and garlic together. Add salt. Sprinkle the cheese, onions, chiles, and shrimp onto the base of the dough and pour over the egg mixture. Bake in a preheated 400° F oven for 30-40 minutes until firm and golden brown. Peel the tail shells off the shrimp and remove the legs and roe if present. Use shrimp to garnish the quiche along with the sprigs of parsley. Serves 6.

Above left: this fascinating photograph from the late 1800s shows a chili stand on the east side of Military Plaza, San Antonio.

46

Riverside Trout

In Tex-Mex cooking fried foods are coated in corn, the indigenous staple grain. Fish dredged in cornmeal is deliciously crisp and sealed. It must, however, be dipped in the cornmeal just before cooking. If it is allowed to stand, the result will be soggy.

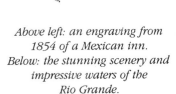

¹/₃-¹/₂ cup vegetable oil
4 Tbsps pine nuts
8 strips bacon, diced
1 cup yellow cornmeal
Pinch salt and white pepper
4 trout weighing about 8 oz each, cleaned
Juice of 1 lime
Fresh sage or coriander

Above left: an engraving from 1854 of a Mexican inn. Below: the stunning scenery and impressive waters of the Rio Grande.

Heat 6 tablespoons of the oil in a large skillet. Add the pine nuts and cook over moderate heat, stirring constantly. When a pale golden brown, remove them with a draining spoon to paper towels. Add the diced bacon to the oil and cook until crisp, stirring constantly. Drain with the pine nuts. Mix the cornmeal, salt and pepper, and dredge the fish well, patting on the cornmeal. Shake off any excess. If necessary, add more oil to the pan – it should come about halfway up the sides of the fish. Re-heat over moderately high heat. When hot, add the fish two at a time and fry until golden brown, about 4-5 minutes. Turn over and reduce the heat slightly if necessary and cook a further 4-5 minutes. Drain and repeat with the remaining fish. Drain almost all the oil from the pan and re-heat the bacon and the nuts very briefly. Add the lime juice and cook a few seconds. Spoon the bacon and pine nut mixture over the fish and garnish with coriander or sage. Serves 4.

CHAPTER FOUR
Meat and Poultry

Above: this evocative photograph from 1879 shows a family from Round Top, Texas, preparing sausages.

*B*eef has always been central to Tex-Mex cuisine, due in part to the reputation and enduring popularity given to it by the cowboy. Barbecued ribs and chili stews are synonymous with Texas, and debate continues as to which is superior. Barbecuing beef over mesquite, and concocting the perfect chili are weighty issues for Texans and tend to overshadow the region's many other popular meat dishes. Lamb, chicken, and pork are all important meats, and both lamb and chicken are particularly suitable partners for fiery Tex-Mex flavors. The astounding growth in the popularity of chicken is attributed to its healthful qualities and the influence of Mexico, where chicken has been the most popular meat since its introduction by the Spanish.

51

Minute Steaks with Taco Sauce

Texas is undoubtedly steak country. Here, the basic steak is given a Tex-Mex sauce to elevate it from the ordinary. Serve with rice or tortillas.

2 Tbsps butter or margarine
2 Tbsps oil
6 minute steaks
Salt and pepper
4 oz button mushrooms, left whole
Full quantity Taco Sauce recipe (see page 30)
Chopped parsley or coriander leaves

Heat the butter or margarine and oil together in a large skillet or sauté pan. Season the steaks with salt and pepper and fry 2 or 3 at a time for 2-3 minutes on each side, or to desired doneness. Remove the steaks to a warm serving dish and add the mushrooms to the pan. Sauté over high heat to brown lightly, remove and keep warm. Drain most of the fat from the pan and pour in the taco sauce. Place over low heat until just bubbling. Spoon over the steaks. Top the steaks with the sautéed mushrooms and sprinkle over parsley or coriander before serving. Serves 6.

Southwestern Stir-Fry

East meets West in a dish that is lightning-fast to cook. Baby corn, traditionally Oriental, echoes the Southwestern love of corn.

1 pound sirloin or rump steak
2 cloves garlic, crushed
6 Tbsps wine vinegar
6 Tbsps oil
Pinch of sugar, salt and pepper
1 bay leaf
1 Tbsp ground cumin
1 small red bell pepper, sliced
1 small green bell pepper, sliced
2 oz baby corn
4 green onions, shredded
Oil for frying

RED SAUCE
4 Tbsps oil
1 medium onion, finely chopped
1-2 green chiles, finely chopped
1-2 cloves garlic, minced
8 fresh ripe tomatoes, peeled, seeded and chopped
6 sprigs fresh coriander
3 Tbsps tomato paste

Slice the meat thinly across the grain. Combine in a plastic bag with the next 6 ingredients. Tie the bag and toss the ingredients inside to coat. Place in a bowl and leave about 4 hours.
Heat the oil for the sauce and cook the onion, chiles, and garlic to soften but not brown. Add remaining sauce ingredients and cook about 15 minutes over gentle heat. Purée in a food processor until smooth. Heat a skillet and add the meat in three batches, discarding the marinade. Cook to brown and set aside. Add about 2 tbsps of oil and cook the bell peppers about 2 minutes. Add the corn and onions and return the meat to the pan. Cook another minute and add the sauce. Cook to heat through and serve immediately. Serves 4.

Above left: fortifications of the Presidio Santa Maria del Loreto de la Bahia, established in 1794, near Goliad.

Chili Roja

Unlike authentic chili, this recipe contains beans. There are countless different recipes for chili, voted the Lone Star State's official dish, and at Terlinga there is even an annual Championship Chili cook-off.

Chili con Carne

This is the basic Tex-Mex chili recipe – of which there are many versions and about which there are many arguments to be had! Chili contests and cook-offs are a Texan phenomenon. Many cooks say no beans, others dispute over the type and quality of meat used, and of course the amount of chile powder used depends on your sense of bravado. Whatever the proportion of ingredients, chili is good served with rice and topped with sour cream, chopped onion, shredded cheese, and diced avocado.

1 Tbsp oil
1 pound ground beef
2 tsps ground cumin
2 tsps mild or hot chile powder
Pinch of oregano
Salt, pepper and pinch sugar
¼ tsp garlic powder
2 Tbsps flour
1 pound canned tomatoes
1 pound canned red kidney beans

Heat the oil in a large saucepan and brown the meat, breaking it up with a fork as it cooks. Sprinkle on the cumin, chile powder, oregano, salt, pepper, sugar, garlic, and flour. Cook, stirring frequently, over

4 Tbsps oil
2 pounds beef chuck, cut into 1-inch pieces
1 large red onion, coarsely chopped
2 cloves garlic, minced
2 red bell peppers, cut into 1-inch pieces
1-2 red chiles, seeded and finely chopped
3 Tbsps mild chile powder
1 Tbsp cumin
1 Tbsp paprika
3 cups beer, water or stock
8 oz canned tomatoes, puréed
2 Tbsps tomato paste
8 oz canned red kidney beans, drained
Pinch of salt
6 ripe tomatoes, peeled, seeded and diced

Pour the oil into a large saucepan or flameproof casserole. When hot, brown the meat in small batches over moderately high heat for about 5 minutes per batch. Set aside the meat on a plate or in the lid of the casserole. Lower the heat and cook the onion, garlic, bell peppers, and chiles for about 5 minutes. Add the chile powder, cumin, and paprika and cook for 1 minute further. Pour on the liquid and add the canned tomatoes, tomato paste, and the meat. Cook slowly for about 1½-2 hours. Add the beans about 45 minutes before the end of cooking time. When the meat is completely tender, add salt to taste and serve garnished with the diced tomatoes. Serves 6-8.

medium heat for about 3 minutes. Add the tomatoes and their liquid and simmer 25-30 minutes. Drain the kidney beans and add just before serving. Heat through about 5 minutes. Serves 4.

Above left: an early illustration of a Mexican household. Above: romanticized in numerous movies, the reality of life for a cowboy is a hard and often lonely existence.

Mexican Chicken & Pepper Salad

A cool lunch for the scorching Tex-Mex summer is given character here by the addition of the local threesome: chile, cayenne, and paprika.

1 pound cooked chicken, cut in strips
½ cup mayonnaise
½ cup plain yogurt
1 tsp chile powder
1 tsp paprika
Pinch of cayenne pepper
½ tsp tomato paste
1 tsp onion paste
1 green bell pepper, finely sliced
1 red bell pepper, finely sliced
6 oz frozen corn, defrosted
6 oz cooked long grain rice, to serve

Place the chicken strips in a large salad bowl. Mix the mayonnaise, yogurt, spices, tomato and onion pastes together and leave to stand briefly for flavors to blend. Fold dressing into the chicken. Add the peppers and corn and mix gently until all the ingredients are coated with dressing. Place the rice on a serving dish and pile the salad into the center. Serve immediately. Serves 6.

Above left: lunch on the 200,000-acre X Ranch near the Davis Mountains, Texas. Left: the Cathedral of Corpus Christi. Right: the Alamo Village, near Bracketville, built as a set for the movie The Alamo.

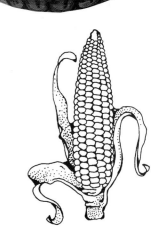

Albondigas (Meatballs)

Mexican Beef Patties

Adding refried beans to the ground beef in this Tex-Mex burger recipe adds flavor and interest, and also helps bind the meat together. Cumin, chile, and garlic are hallmarks of this region's cooking, and bring these patties alive. They are good served with taco sauce, an avocado and tomato salad and warm flour tortillas.

1 onion, finely chopped
1 Tbsp oil
12 oz ground beef
8 oz canned refried beans
4 Tbsps bread crumbs
½ tsp cumin
1 tsp chile powder
1 clove garlic, minced
Salt and pepper
1 egg, beaten
Flour to coat
Oil for deep frying
Watercress, to garnish

Cook the onion in the oil until soft but not browned. Mix in the beef, beans, bread crumbs, spices, garlic, and seasoning and gradually add the egg until the mixture holds together well. Turn the mixture out onto a well-floured surface and divide into 8 pieces. Shape into

Taco sauce on these spicy meatballs gives this dish a double dose of Tex-Mex flavor, and they are well complemented with rice, refried beans or guacamole.

8 oz ground veal
8 oz ground beef
1 clove garlic, crushed
2 Tbsps dry bread crumbs
½ chile, seeded and finely chopped
½ tsp ground cumin
Salt
1 egg, beaten
Flour, to coat
Oil for frying
Full quantity Taco Sauce recipe (see page 30)
2 green onions, chopped

Mix together the veal, beef, garlic, bread crumbs, chile, cumin, salt, and egg until well blended. Add the egg gradually. Turn the mixture out onto a floured surface and divide into 16 equal pieces. With floured hands, shape the mixture into balls. Pour about 3 tablespoons of oil into a large skillet and place over high heat. When the oil is hot, place in the meatballs and fry for 5-10 minutes until brown on all sides. Turn frequently during cooking. Remove the browned meatballs and drain well on paper towels. Place in an ovenproof dish and pour over the taco sauce. Heat through in a preheated 350° F oven for 10 minutes. Sprinkle with chopped green onions to serve.
Serves 4.

even-sized patties with well-floured hands. Knead the pieces before shaping, if necessary, to make sure mixture holds together with no cracks. Coat lightly with flour and refrigerate until firm. Pour enough oil into a large skillet to completely cover the patties. Fry 2 at a time until golden brown on all sides and completely cooked through. Remove from the oil and drain on paper towels. Arrange on a serving plate and garnish with watercress.
Serves 4.

Above left: a Mexican wagon train loading up in Main Street, San Antonio.

58

Spare Ribs in Chile & Cream Sauce

Barbecued Ribs

Barbecued meats served with a sweet and spicy sauce are good eaten in the Texan/Mexican borderlands where warm, sultry evenings provide the perfect excuse for eating outside. Here, the meat is prepared in the oven for year-round convenience. Serve with warm tortillas and Spicy Rice and Beans.

4½ pounds pork spare ribs

SAUCE
*1 cup tomato ketchup
2 tsps mustard powder
4 Tbsps Worcestershire sauce
2 Tbsps vinegar
4 Tbsps brown sugar
½ chile, seeded and finely chopped
½ a small onion, finely chopped
4 Tbsps water
Salt (if necessary)*

Place the ribs in a roasting pan and cover with foil. Cook for 15 minutes at 425° F. Meanwhile, combine all the sauce ingredients in a heavy-based pan and bring to a boil. Reduce heat and simmer for about 15 minutes. Reduce the oven temperature to 350° F and uncover the ribs. Pour over the sauce and bake a further hour, basting

Cocoa and chiles seem unlikely partners, but it is authentic Tex-Mex, borrowed from Mexico where the bitter cocoa bean has been used for centuries as a valued spice that adds color, depth and flavor. These sophisticated ribs can be cooked on an outdoor barbecue for the last 30 minutes.

*2¼ pounds spare ribs
1 tsp unsweetened cocoa
1 Tbsp flour
½ tsp cumin
½ tsp chile powder
½ tsp dried oregano, crushed
Salt and pepper
1 cup warm water
2 Tbsps thin honey
2 Tbsps heavy cream
Lime wedges and watercress for garnish*

*Leave the ribs in whole slabs, put in a roasting pan and cook in a 400° F oven for 20-25 minutes, or until well browned. Drain off all the excess fat. Blend together the cocoa, flour, cumin, chile powder, oregano, seasoning, water, and honey and pour over the ribs. Lower the temperature to 350° F and cook ribs for a further 30 minutes, until the sauce has reduced and the ribs are tender. Cut the ribs into pieces and arrange on a serving dish. Pour the cream into the sauce in the roasting pan and place over moderate heat. Bring to a boil and pour over the ribs. Garnish with lime wedges and watercress and serve with rice and an avocado or tomato salad.
Serves 4.*

frequently. Remove the ribs from the roasting pan and reserve the sauce. Place the ribs on a cutting board and slice into individual rib pieces, between the bones. Skim any fat from the surface of the sauce and serve the sauce separately. Serves 6.

*Above left: the barber shop at the East Texas Oil Museum in Kilgore. The museum recreates many aspects of life in the oil boom days of the 1930s
Above: the much-prized Texas longhorn.*

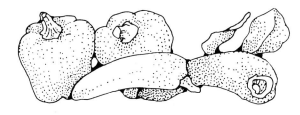

Chicken with Red Peppers

The warm taste of roasted red peppers is typically Tex-Mex. Sage is a very common herb in the Southwestern United States. If unavailable fresh, substitute coriander or parsley leaves as a garnish.

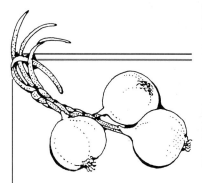

4 large red bell peppers
Oil
4 skinned and boned chicken breasts
Salt and pepper
1 clove garlic, finely chopped
3 Tbsps white wine vinegar
2 green onions, finely chopped
Sage leaves for garnish

Cut the bell peppers in half and remove the stems, cores and seeds. Flatten the peppers with the palm of your hand and brush the skin sides lightly with oil. Place the peppers skin side up on the rack of a preheated broiler and cook about 2 inches away from the heat source until the skins are well blistered and charred. Wrap the peppers in a clean towel and allow them to stand until cool. Peel off the skins with a small vegetable knife. Cut into thin strips and set aside.

Place the chicken breasts between two sheets of wax paper and flatten by hitting with a rolling pin or meat mallet. Heat $1\frac{1}{2}$ tablespoons of oil in a large skillet. Season the chicken breasts with salt and pepper on both sides and place in the hot oil. Cook 5 minutes, turn over and cook until tender and lightly browned. Remove the chicken and keep it warm. Add the pepper strips, garlic, vinegar, and green onions to the pan and cook briefly until the vinegar loses its strong aroma. Slice the chicken breasts across the grain into $\frac{1}{4}$-inch thick slices and arrange on serving plates. Spoon the pan juices over the chicken. Arrange the pepper mixture with the chicken and garnish with the sage leaves. Serves 4.

Right: although the Texan economy is now dominated by oil and computers, cattle ranching remains a vital social and economic force.

Leg of Lamb with Chile Sauce

Here familiar Tex-Mex spices – cayenne, cumin, paprika – are mixed with cocoa, which is used not as a sweetening but as a seasoning as was traditional in pre-Columbian Mexico. You do not notice a chocolate flavor in this dish, the cocoa rather adds a depth and richness to the sauce.

2¼-pound leg of lamb

MARINADE
1 tsp unsweetened cocoa
¼ tsp cayenne pepper
½ tsp ground cumin
½ tsp paprika
½ tsp ground oregano
½ cup water
½ cup orange juice
½ cup red wine
1 clove of garlic, minced
2 Tbsps light brown sugar
Pinch of salt
1 Tbsp cornstarch
Orange slices and coriander, to garnish

If the lamb has a lot of surface fat, trim slightly with a sharp knife. If possible, remove the paper-thin skin on the outside of the lamb. Place lamb in a shallow dish. Mix together the marinade ingredients, except cornstarch, and pour over the lamb, turning it well to coat completely. Cover and refrigerate for 12–24 hours, turning occasionally.

Drain the lamb, reserving the marinade, and place in a roasting pan. Cook in a preheated 350° F oven for about 2 hours until meat is cooked according to taste. Baste occasionally with the marinade and pan juices. Remove lamb to a serving dish and keep warm. Skim the fat from the top of the roasting pan with a large spoon and discard. Pour remaining marinade into the pan juices in the roasting pan and bring to a boil, stirring to loosen the sediment. Mix cornstarch with a small amount of water and add some of the liquid from the roasting pan. Gradually stir cornstarch mixture into the pan and bring back to a boil. Cook, stirring constantly, until thickened and clear. Add more orange juice, wine or water as necessary. Garnish the lamb with orange slices and sprigs of coriander. Pour over some of the sauce and serve the rest separately. Serves 4.

Above: Sidbury House in Heritage Park, a plaza of restored and relocated turn-of-the-century houses in Corpus Christi.

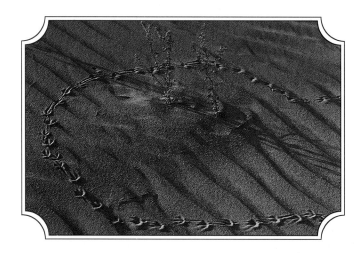

Mexican Kebabs

These delicious Tex-Mex kebabs marry Texan barbecue cooking with the ancient Mexican spice combination of bitter cocoa and biting chiles.

1 pound pork or lamb, cut into 2-inch pieces
4 oz large button mushrooms, left whole
8 bay leaves
1 tsp unsweetened cocoa
2 tsps chile powder
1/4 tsp garlic powder
1/2 tsp dried marjoram
Salt and pepper
6 Tbsps oil
2 medium onions, quartered
6 oz cooked rice, to serve
1/2 quantity Taco Sauce recipe (see page 30)

Place meat and mushrooms in a bowl. Add the bay leaves, cocoa, chile powder, garlic powder, marjoram, and seasoning to the oil and stir into the meat and mushrooms to coat. Cover the bowl and leave to marinate at least 6 hours, preferably overnight. Remove meat, mushrooms and bay leaves from the marinade and reserve it. Thread onto skewers, alternating meat, onions, mushrooms, and bay leaves. Place under a preheated broiler for 15-20 minutes, turning frequently until cooked to desired doneness. If using pork, the meat must be thoroughly cooked and not served pink. Baste with reserved marinade. Mix hot rice with taco sauce and spoon onto a warm serving dish. Place the kebabs on top of the rice to serve. Serves 4.

Above left: only the birds disturb the peace at Monahans Sandhills State Park, a hazardous barrier that once hampered many wagon trains heading across the state. Above: dipping sheep in Southwest Texas. Left: the old post office near Hot Springs, Big Bend National Park.

Barbecued Pork Stew

Bell pepper, chile powder and Tabasco sauce turn this pork stew into a really spicy Tex-Mex dish. Serve with warm tortillas and Spicy Rice and Beans.

Chili Verde

This is a green version of the Texan classic "bowl of red." Generally in Tex-Mex cooking a chili has come to mean a meat and chile pepper stew. There are many variations and Texan cooks pride themselves on their own chili recipes. Serve this for lunch or a light supper with warm tortillas.

Oil
2 pounds lean pork, cut into 1-inch pieces
3 green bell peppers, cut into 1-inch pieces
1-2 green chiles, seeded and finely chopped
1 small bunch green onions, chopped
2 cloves garlic, minced
2 tsps ground cumin
2 tsps chopped fresh oregano
3 Tbsps chopped fresh coriander
1 bay leaf
3 cups beer, water or chicken stock
8 oz canned chickpeas, drained
1½ Tbsps cornstarch mixed with 3 Tbsps cold water (optional)
Salt
1 large ripe avocado, peeled and diced
1 Tbsp lime juice

Oil
2 pounds pork shoulder, cut in 2-inch cubes
2 medium onions, cut in 2-inch pieces
1 large green bell pepper, cut in 2-inch pieces
1 Tbsp chile powder
2 cloves garlic, minced
1 pound canned tomatoes
3 Tbsps tomato paste
1 Tbsp Worcestershire sauce
½ cup water or beef stock
2 Tbsps cider vinegar
1 bay leaf
½ tsp dried oregano
Salt and a few drops Tabasco sauce

Heat about 2 tablespoons of oil in a large sauté pan or skillet. When hot, add the pork cubes in two batches. Brown over high heat for about 5 minutes per batch. Remove to a plate. Add more oil if necessary and cook the onions and peppers to soften slightly. Add the chile powder and garlic and cook 1 minute more. Add the tomatoes, their juice, and the tomato paste. Stir in the Worcestershire sauce, water or stock, and vinegar, breaking up the tomatoes slightly. Add bay leaf, oregano, and salt. Transfer to a flameproof casserole dish. Bring the mixture to a boil, cover, and then cook slowly for about 1½ hours. When the meat is completely tender, skim any fat from the surface of the sauce, remove the bay leaf and add a few drops of Tabasco sauce to taste. Adjust salt and serve. Serves 4.

Heat 4 tablespoons of oil in a large flameproof casserole and lightly brown the pork cubes over high heat. Lower the heat, add the bell peppers and cook to soften slightly. Add the chiles, onions, garlic, and cumin and cook for 2 minutes. Add the herbs and liquid and reduce the heat. Simmer, covered, 1-1½ hours or until the meat is tender. Add the chickpeas during the last 45 minutes.
If necessary, thicken with the cornstarch, stirring constantly after adding until the liquid thickens and clears. Add salt to taste and remove the bay leaf. Toss the avocado in lime juice and sprinkle over the top of the chili to serve. Serves 6-8.

Above left: futuristic office blocks are in marked contrast to the "pioneer village" in Dallas' Old City Park.

CHAPTER FIVE
Snacks and Side dishes

Above: a cowboy moves a herd of working horses on to the next camp on the ranch.

*T*ex-Mex cooking features numerous lively snacks and side dishes, from the traditional favorites such as refried beans, to spicy, sophisticated salads. Beans were once an invaluable part of the diet of cattlemen who ate red, lima or pinto beans stewed into an unappetizing, if nutritive, mush and served with cornbread or biscuits. A more recent rise in status has been accorded to salads. At one time the only sight of a salad would have been sprinkled over the top of tacos, but today's health-conscious cooks have devised many delicious salads using some favorite Tex-Mex ingredients, but adding some lighter ingredients such as endive and pine nuts.

Refried Beans

This is a classic Mexican and Tex-Mex dish, both in its own right served with tortillas – as here, or as an accompaniment to poultry, meat or vegetable recipes.

8 oz dried pinto beans
Water, to cover
1 bay leaf
6 Tbsps oil
Salt and pepper
Shredded mild cheese
Shredded lettuce
Tortillas

Soak the beans overnight. Change the water, add the ba
leaf and bring to a boil. Cover and simmer about 2
hours, or until the beans are completely tender.
Alternatively, bring the beans to a boil in cold water and
then allow to boil rapidly for 10 minutes. Cover and
leave to stand for 1 hour. Change the water and then
continue with the recipe. Drain the beans and reserve a
small amount of the cooking liquid. Discard bay leaf.
Heat the oil in a heavy skillet. Add the beans and, as they
fry, mash them with the back of a spoon. Do not
overmash – about a third of the beans should stay whole.
Season to taste. Smooth out the beans in the pan and
cook until the bottom is set but not browned. Turn the
beans over and cook the other side. Top with the cheese
and cook the beans until the cheese melts. Serve with
finely shredded lettuce and tortillas, either warm or cut
in triangles and deep-fried until crisp. Serves 6-8.

Tostadas

Tex-Mex cooking encompasses a great variety of "finger foods," such as these tostadas. The Tex-Mex cook has great flexibility to experiment with different fillings and toppings, and the number of chiles used!

1 pound ground beef or pork
2 tsps oil
2 tsps chile powder
1 tsp ground cumin
1 tsp ground coriander
3/4-1 1/2 cups refried beans
12 tostada shells

TOPPINGS
Shredded lettuce
Shredded cheddar cheese
Tomatoes, seeded and chopped
Sour cream
Olives
Cooked shrimp
Green onions, chopped
Taco Sauce (see page 30)

Cook the meat in the oil in a
medium skillet. Sprinkle on the
spices and cook quickly to brown.
Reheat the beans and place the
tostada shells on a baking sheet.

Heat 2-3 minutes in a moderate
oven. Spread 1-2 tablespoons of the
beans on each tostada shell. Top
each shell with some of the beef
mixture. Add the topping
ingredients in different
combinations and serve
immediately. Serves 12.

*Above left: an early illustration
of a wealthy household in
Monterey, once considered the
social center of Northern Mexico.
Right: the rustic simplicity of a
ranch dining room.*

Spicy Rice and Beans

Rice and beans are natural Tex-Mex partners, especially when spiced with bell pepper, cumin and coriander. This can be served with warm tortillas and a salad, or as a side dish with enchiladas, meat or poultry.

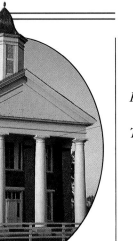

Above left: Guadalupe Mountains National Park.
Left: Old Nacodoches University, built in 1858.

4 Tbsps oil
2 cups long grain rice
1 onion, finely chopped
1 green bell pepper, chopped
1 tsp each ground cumin and coriander
1-2 tsps Tabasco
Salt
3½ cups stock
1 pound canned red kidney beans, drained and rinsed
1 pound tomatoes, drained and coarsely chopped
Chopped parsley

Heat the oil in a casserole or a large, deep saucepan. Add the rice and cook until just turning opaque. Add the onion, bell pepper, and cumin and coriander. Cook gently for a further 2 minutes. Add the Tabasco, salt, stock, and beans and bring to a boil. Cover and cook about 45 minutes, or until the rice is tender and most of the liquid is absorbed. Remove from the heat and add the tomatoes, stirring them in gently. Leave to stand, covered, for 5 minutes. Fluff up the mixture with a fork and sprinkle with parsley to serve. Serves 6-8.

PARSLEY

Salad Huevos Rancheros

Originally a cowboy dish consisting of just eggs, chorizo and green onions, this more sophisticated version is now a Tex-Mex appetizer.

1 large red bell pepper, roasted (see Chicken with Red Peppers page 62)
1 chorizo sausage
4 heads Belgian endive
1 large or 2 small zucchini, cut into matchstick pieces
1 small jicama, cut into matchstick pieces
2-3 green onions, shredded
4 Tbsps pine nuts
4 eggs
1 tsp chopped fresh coriander

DRESSING
6 Tbsps oil
2 Tbsps lime juice
Dash of Tabasco
Salt and pinch of sugar

Prepare the roasted bell pepper and cut it into thin strips. Bring a pan of water to a boil, add the chorizo and simmer for about 8 minutes until tender. Peel the casing off the chorizo while warm and cut the meat into thin strips. Separate the leaves of the endive and slice or leave whole if small. Bring water to a boil and blanch the zucchini and jicama strips for 1 minute. Rinse under cold water until completely cool and leave to drain. Combine with the endive and green onion. Add the strips of chorizo and set aside. Toast the pine nuts in a moderate oven until golden brown – about 5 minutes. Bring at least 2 inches of water to a boil in a skillet or sauté pan. Turn down the heat to simmering. Break an egg onto a saucer or into a cup. Stir the water to make a whirlpool and then carefully pour the egg into the center, keeping the saucer or cup close to the level of the water. When the water stops swirling and the white begins to set, gently move the egg over to the side and repeat with each remaining egg. Cook the eggs until the whites are completely set, but the yolks are still soft. Remove the eggs from the water with a draining spoon and place them immediately into a bowl of cold water.

Mix the dressing ingredients together and pour half over the vegetables and sausage. Toss to coat. Arrange the mixture on individual plates in the shape of nests. Remove the eggs from the cold water with the draining spoon and hold them over a towel for a few minutes to drain completely. Place one egg in the middle of each nest. Spoon the remaining dressing over each egg, sprinkle over the pine nuts and garnish the yolk with chopped coriander. Serves 4.

Above: a scene from 1885 of the historic fountain in the Plaza Santo Domingo, Mexico City. Right: the largest park in the Lone Star State, Big Bend National Park covers more than 700,000 acres and is a haven for backpackers and nature lovers.

Churros

*These fritters can be either sweet or savory. Either way,
they're a treat with a Mexican influence.*

BASIC DOUGH
*Scant 1 cup water plus 2 Tbsps
3 Tbsps butter or margarine
Pinch of salt
1 cup all-purpose flour
6 Tbsps cornmeal
2 eggs
Oil for deep frying*

SAVORY INGREDIENTS
*2 Tbsps finely shredded cheese
2 chiles, seeded and finely chopped
Parmesan cheese (optional)*

SWEET INGREDIENTS
*4 Tbsps sugar
1 Tbsp unsweetened cocoa
1 tsp ground cinnamon
Powdered sugar (optional)*

*Combine the water, butter or margarine, and salt in a
heavy-based saucepan. If making sweet churros, add
sugar as well. Cook over medium heat until the butter or
margarine melts. Immediately stir in the flour and
cornmeal. Keeping the pan over medium heat, stir until
the mixture pulls away from the sides of the pan and
forms a ball. Take off the heat and cool slightly. Add the
eggs one at a time, beating vigorously in between each
addition. It may not be necessary to add all the egg. Beat
until the mixture is smooth and shiny and thick enough
to pipe. Add the cheese and chiles or the cocoa and
cinnamon with the eggs. Spoon the mixture into a pastry
bag fitted with a star tip.
Heat the oil in a deep-fat fryer, deep saucepan or deep
sauté pan to a depth of at least 4 inches. Pipe the dough
into the oil in 10-inch strips and fry until golden brown,
about 3 minutes per side. As the churros cook in the hot
fat, they will curl into different shapes. Drain on paper
towels and sprinkle the savory churros with Parmesan
cheese and the sweet with powdered sugar, if desired.
Serve warm. Makes 12-14.*

*Above: this 1925 photograph
shows a young resident of San
Antonio baking a cake for
needy fellow citizens.*

Moyettes

This is a Tex-Mex brunch dish which can be prepared in advance and heated through just before serving.

4 crusty rolls
2 Tbsps butter or margarine
8 oz canned refried beans
2 green onions, chopped
4 Tbsps shredded Tilsit cheese

Cut the rolls in half and remove some of the inside. Soften the butter and spread on both sides of the rolls. Fill the rolls with the refried beans. Sprinkle with the green onion and top with the shredded cheese. Place the rolls on a cookie sheet and cook in a preheated 325° F oven for 15-20 minutes, or until the cheese has melted and the beans are hot. Serve immediately. Serves 4.

Nachos

These make excellent Tex-Mex cocktail savories. It is best to make them at the last minute as tortilla chips become soggy if topped too soon before serving.

1 package round tortilla chips
1 can refried beans
Full quantity Taco Sauce recipe (see page 30)
1 can Jalapeño bean dip
8-10 cherry tomatoes, sliced
½ cup sour cream or plain yogurt
Sliced black and stuffed green olives
Shredded cheddar cheese

TACO FILLING
2 tsps oil
8 oz ground beef
2 tsps chili powder
Pinch of ground coriander
Pinch of cayenne pepper
Salt and pepper

Prepare taco filling as for Tacos recipe. Top half of the tortilla chips with refried beans and half with beef taco filling. Place a spoonful of taco sauce on the bean-topped chips and Jalapeño bean dip in the beef-topped chips. Top the tortilla chips with tomatoes, sour cream or yogurt, olives or cheese in any desired combination, and serve. Serves 8-10.

Above left: San Antonio market place in 1883. Above: the Spanish Govenor's Palace in San Antonio, built in 1749, once housed the officials of the Spanish Province of Texas.

Denver Omelet

This is a good one-pan cowboy recipe. If prepared like scrambled eggs, the mixture can double as a tortilla filling.

4 strips bacon, diced
½ small onion, chopped
½ small green bell pepper, chopped
1 tomato, seeded and diced
3 eggs, beaten
Salt and pepper
1 Tbsp shredded cheese
Dash Tabasco (optional)
Chopped parsley, to garnish

Heat a medium-size skillet or omelet pan. Add the bacon and sauté slowly until the fat is rendered. Turn up the heat and cook until the bacon begins to brown and crisp. Add the onion and bell pepper and cook to soften and finish off the bacon. Mix the tomato with the eggs, salt, pepper, cheese, and Tabasco, if using. Pour into the pan and stir once or twice with a fork to mix all the ingredients. Cook until lightly browned on the underside. Place under a pre-heated broiler and cook the top quickly until brown and slightly puffy. Sprinkle with parsley, cut into wedges, and serve immediately.
Serves 2.

Above left: the Swedish Log Cabin in Zilker Park, Austin. Above: the spectacular view across Chisos Basin, in Big Bend National Park.

CHAPTER SIX
Desserts

*Above: the authentically-furnished Spanish
Governor's Palace in San Antonio, built in 1749.*

*D*esserts are an important feature of any Tex-Mex
meal as they help to extinguish the heat of a
spicy main course with a cool or sweet finale.
Chocolate flans are one of the most popular desserts
and it is, in fact, the Aztecs who are credited with
popularizing the cocoa bean and turning it into an
extremely strong chocolate drink, although it was a
long time before it became the chocolate we know
and love today. Other popular desserts include
watermelon, fresh fruit salads, syrup-poached fruit,
and, of course, ice creams and fruit ices. All of these
provide the perfect method for dusting down and
refreshing the taste buds until the next round of
savory delights.

Black Bottom Ice Cream Pie

Fruit Empanadas

Tortillas when stuffed and deep-fried become empanadas.

Full quantity Tortilla recipe (see page 26)
Oil, for deep frying
10 ripe fresh apricots, halved and pitted, or 1 pound canned apricots, well drained
1 pound cream cheese
Powdered sugar

Prepare the tortilla dough, roll out into 10 tortillas but do not pre-cook. Heat oil in a deep saucepan, sauté pan or deep-fat fryer to a depth of at least 2 inches. Oil should reach a temperature of 375° F. Cut the apricots into quarters and the cheese into 10 even pieces. Place one piece of cheese and an even amount of apricots on the lower half of each tortilla. Fold over the upper half and seal the edges. Crimp tightly into a decorative pattern. Fry one empanada at a time until golden on both sides. Baste the upper side frequently with oil to make the tortilla dough puffy. Drain well on paper towels and serve warm, sprinkled with powdered sugar.

Black Bottom Ice Cream Pie

This area of border cooking is all about strong, positive flavors and indulgence, which is easy when local products include coffee, cocoa, coconut and rum.

8-10 Graham crackers, crushed
½ cup butter or margarine, melted
4 oz shredded coconut
2 oz semi-sweet chocolate, melted
3 cups coffee ice cream
Dark rum (optional)

Crush crackers with a rolling pin or in a food processor. Mix with melted butter or margarine. Press into an 8½-inch deep loose-bottom pie pan. Chill thoroughly in the refrigerator. Meanwhile, combine 4 tablespoons of the coconut with the melted chocolate. When cooled but not solidified, add about a quarter of the coffee ice cream, mixing well. Spread the mixture on the base of the crust and freeze until firm. Soften the remaining ice cream with an electric mixer or food processor and spread over the chocolate-coconut layer. Re-freeze until firm. Toast the remaining coconut in a moderate oven, stirring frequently until pale golden brown. Allow to cool completely. Remove the pie from the freezer and leave in the refrigerator 30 minutes before serving. Push up the base of the pan and place the pie on a serving plate. Sprinkle the top with toasted coconut. Cut into wedges and drizzle with rum before serving.

Mango Fool

Mangoes, laced with ginger and lime, offer a wonderful taste of Mexico and a soothing coolness ideal to placate the palate following a fiery Texan chili.

2 ripe mangoes
1 small piece ginger root, peeled, and shredded
1 cup powdered sugar, sifted
Juice of ½ a lime
½ cup heavy cream

Cut the mangoes in half, cutting around the stone. Scoop out the pulp into a blender or food processor. Reserve two slices. Add the ginger, powdered sugar, and lime juice and purée in the blender or food processor until smooth. Whip the cream until soft peaks form and fold into the mango purée. Divide the mixture between 6 glass serving dishes and refrigerate for 1 hour before serving. Cut the reserved mango slices into 6 smaller slices or pieces and decorate the fools. Serves 6.

Above left: the hectic days following the discovery of the huge East Texas Oil Field in 1930 is recreated at the Oil Museum in Kilgore.

Tropical Fruit Salad

Guava Mint Sorbet

The stimulating combination of guava and mint is very typical of the exotic Tex-Mex range of piquant tastes.

⅔ cup granulated sugar
1 cup water
4 ripe guavas
2 Tbsps chopped fresh mint
Juice of 1 lime
1 egg white
Fresh mint leaves, to decorate

Combine the sugar and water in a heavy-based saucepan and bring slowly to a boil to dissolve the sugar. When the mixture is a clear syrup, boil rapidly for 30 seconds. Allow to cool to room temperature and then chill in the refrigerator. Cut the guavas in half and scoop out the pulp. Discard the peels and seeds and purée the fruit until smooth in a food processor. Add the mint and combine with cold syrup. Add lime juice until the right balance of sweetness is reached. Pour the mixture into a shallow container and freeze until slushy. Process again to break up ice crystals and then freeze until firm. Whip the egg white until stiff but not dry. Process the sorbet again and when smooth,

Tex-Mex cooking offers a feast of succulent fruits which continue the theme of strong vibrant flavors so characteristic of this part of the world. A splash of tequila adds sophistication and an even greater authenticity to this fruit salad.

½ cantaloupe or honeydew melon, cubed or made into balls
½ small fresh pineapple, peeled, cored and cubed or sliced
4 oz fresh strawberries, hulled and halved (leave whole, if small)
1 mango, peeled and sliced or cubed
8 oz watermelon, seeded and cubed
4 oz guava or papaya, peeled and cubed
2 oranges, peeled and segmented
1 prickly pear, peeled and sliced (optional)
½ cup sugar
½ cup water
Grated rind and juice of 1 lemon
2 Tbsps chopped pecans, to garnish (optional)

Mix the prepared fruit together in a bowl. Dissolve the sugar in the water over gentle heat and when the mixture is no longer grainy, leave it to cool completely. Add lemon rind and juice to the sugar syrup and pour over the prepared fruit. Refrigerate well before serving. Sprinkle with chopped nuts, if desired. Serves 6.

add the egg white. Mix once or twice and then freeze again until firm. Remove from the freezer 15 minutes before serving and keep in the refrigerator. Scoop out and garnish each serving with mint leaves. Makes 3 cups.

Above left: the Law Office in Sam Houston Memorial Park, Huntsville. Right: a fascinating recreation of a 1930s store.

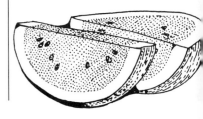

Mexican Chocolate Flan

Flan in Mexico means a custard mold. Cacao beans, an important Tex-Mex ingredient, are native to southern Mexico and were imported by the Aztecs into central Mexico where they were so valued they were used as a form of currency, and later to make chocolate – an Aztec word – which they drank as a stimulating, energy-rich drink. Cinnamon, which is combined with chocolate here, is also a traditional Tex-Mex flavor.

½ cup sugar
2 Tbsps water
Juice of ½ a lemon
2 oz semi-sweet chocolate
1 cup milk
1 cinnamon stick
2 whole eggs
2 egg yolks
4 Tbsps sugar

Combine the first amount of sugar with the water and lemon juice in a small, heavy-based saucepan. Cook over gentle heat until the sugar starts to dissolve. Swirl the pan from time to time, but don't stir. Once the sugar liquifies, bring the syrup to a boil and cook until golden brown. While preparing the syrup, heat 4 custard cups in a 350° F oven. When the syrup is ready, pour into the cups and swirl to coat the sides and base evenly. Leave to cool at room temperature.

Chop the chocolate into small pieces and heat with the milk and cinnamon, stirring occasionally to help the chocolate dissolve. Whisk the whole eggs and the yolks together with the remaining sugar until slightly frothy. Gradually whisk in the chocolate milk. Remove the cinnamon stick. Pour the chocolate custard carefully into the custard cups and place them in a roasting pan of hand-hot water. Place the roasting pan in the oven and bake the custards until just slightly wobbly in the center – about 20-30 minutes. Cool at room temperature and refrigerate for several hours or overnight before serving. Loosen custards carefully from the sides of the dishes and invert into serving plates. Shake to allow custards to drop out. Serves 4.

Frozen Lime and Blueberry Cream

Blueberries grow wild in this part of the United States and recipes using them abound.

Juice and rind of 4 limes
Water
1 cup sugar
4 oz blueberries
3 egg whites
1 cup heavy cream, whipped

Measure the lime juice and make up to 6 tablespoons with water if necessary. Combine with the sugar in a heavy-based pan and bring to a boil slowly to dissolve the sugar. When the mixture forms a clear syrup, boil rapidly to 250° F on a candy thermometer. Meanwhile, combine the blueberries with about 4 tablespoons water in a small saucepan. Bring to a boil and then simmer, covered, until very soft. Purée, sieve to remove the seeds and skin, and set aside to cool. Whisk the egg whites until stiff but not dry and then pour on the hot sugar syrup in a steady stream, whisking constantly. Add the rind and allow the meringue to cool. When cold,

fold in the whipped cream. Pour in the purée and marble through the mixture with a rubber spatula. Do not over-fold. Pour the mixture into a lightly-oiled mold or bowl and freeze until firm. To serve, dip the mold for about 10 seconds in hot water. Place a plate over the bottom of the mold, invert and shake to turn out. Decorate with extra whipped cream, blueberries or lime slices. Serves 6.

Chocolate Cinnamon Monkey Bread

Cocoa and cinnamon both appear in early accounts of Mexican cooking, and indeed when these ingredients were roasted together with chiles this was the first way in which cocoa appears to have been eaten.

DOUGH
1 Tbsp sugar
1 package dry yeast
4 Tbsps warm water
3-3¾ cups bread flour
6 Tbsps sugar
Pinch of salt
5 Tbsps butter, softened
5 eggs

TOPPING
1 cup sugar
2 tsps cinnamon
2 tsps unsweetened cocoa
6 Tbsps finely chopped pecans
½ cup butter, melted

Sprinkle 1 tablespoon sugar and the yeast on top of the water and leave it in a warm place until foaming. Sift 3 cups of flour into a bowl and add the sugar and salt. Cut in the butter until completely blended. Add 2 eggs and the yeast mixture, mixing in well. Add the remaining eggs one at a time until the mixture forms a soft, spongy dough. Add remaining flour as necessary. Knead for 10 minutes on a lightly floured surface until smooth and elastic. Place the dough in a greased bowl and turn over to grease all the surfaces. Cover with plastic wrap and put in a warm place. Leave to stand for 1-1½ hours or until doubled in bulk.
Butter a ring mold liberally. Punch down the dough and knead it again for about 5 minutes. Shape into balls about 2 inches in diameter. Mix the topping ingredients together except for the melted butter. Roll the dough balls in the butter and then in the sugar mixture. Place a layer of dough balls in the bottom of the mold and continue until all the dough and topping has been used. Cover and allow to rise again about 15 minutes. Bake in a pre-heated 350° F oven for about 45-50 minutes. Loosen from the pan and turn out while still warm. Pull this bread apart to serve in individual pieces rather than slicing it. Serve warm with coffee or tea, or serve as an accompaniment to a fresh fruit salad.

Above: southwest Texas is perfect hiking country noted for its spectacular views and varied plant and animal life.

Index

Acknowledgements

The publishers would like to thank the following organizations and individuals
for contributing to this book: The Institute of Texan Cultures, San Antonio,
Texas; San Antonio Conservation Society; U.T. The Institute of Texan Cultures,
The San Antonio Light Collection; Zeva Olebaum; Sue Philpot; Louisa Vernay.